HOW TO BECOME A GOOD CITIZEN OF THE UNITED STATES

(Guide To Becoming A Good Citizen)

JONATHAN SCOTT

ACKNOWLEDGEMEN

I extend my heartfelt gratitude to Jonathan Scott for his exemplary commitment to being a model citizen of the United States and for sharing his invaluable insights in the book "How to Become a Good Citizen of the United States."

Jonathan's unwavering dedication to civic responsibility serves as an inspiration to us all. His book not only chronicles his personal journey but also provides a comprehensive guide on fostering positive citizenship traits. Through its pages, readers are empowered with the knowledge and motivation to actively engage in their communities, promoting unity and understanding.

I commend Jonathan for his efforts in bridging diverse perspectives and encouraging individuals to contribute meaningfully to the well-being of our nation. His book stands as a beacon, guiding us towards a collective understanding of the responsibilities we bear as citizens.

May this acknowledgment serve as a tribute to Jonathan Scott's impactful work and as a reminder of the enduring importance of cultivating good citizenship for the betterment of our great nation.

INTRODUCTION

Becoming a good citizen of the United States takes hard work, dedication, and a sense of civic responsibility. There are many things a person can do to become a good citizen, from taking part in civic activities to paying taxes to maintaining a healthy lifestyle. Here are some tips on becoming a good citizen of the United States.

<u>GUIDE TO BECOMING A GOOD CITIZEN</u>

The guide to becoming a good citizen of the United States is "participation." Being an active participant in your community, understanding and upholding the laws, being knowledgeable about your rights and responsibilities, and embracing the principles of equality, freedom, and democracy are essential for being a good citizen of the United States. Additionally, respecting the diversity of the nation and contributing positively to the betterment of society are also crucial aspects of being a good citizen. By actively engaging in civic duties, respecting others, and working towards the common good, individuals can embody the qualities of a good citizen in the United States.

1. *Respect the rights, beliefs and opinions of others*
2. *Support and defend the Constitution*
3. *Respect and obey federal, state, and local laws*
4. *Participate in the democratic process*
5. *Pay income and other taxes honestly, and on time*
6. *Serve on juries when called upon*

7. *Serve in the military or defense forces when needed*

8. *Respect the flag and national anthem*

9. *Vote in local, state, and national elections*

10. *Respect the national symbols of the United States*

11. *Be informed about the issues and participate in civil discourse*

12. *Volunteer in causes which are important to you*

13. *Be informed about the history, cultures, and customs of the United States*

14.   And lastly, be a good neighbor and participate in your community

<u>CHAPTER 1</u>

Respect The Rights, Beliefs And Opinions Of Others:

It is a foundational principle for a harmonious and just society. It is a reminder that each person is entitled to their own perspective, and it is important to approach others with empathy and understanding, even when their views differ from our own.

Respecting the rights of others means acknowledging and honoring the liberties and freedoms that belong to every individual. This encompasses the right to express oneself, the right to personal autonomy, and the right to be treated fairly and justly within the legal system. Respecting these rights involves refraining from actions that infringe upon them and actively working to protect and uphold them.

Beliefs and opinions are deeply personal and often tied to an individual's identity and experiences. Recognizing and respecting the diversity of beliefs and opinions means understanding that not everyone will think or feel the same way about a given issue. It involves engaging in open, constructive dialogue, seeking common ground, and embracing the opportunity to learn from others.

At its core, respecting the rights, beliefs, and opinions of others is about fostering a culture of inclusivity and compassion. It is about creating an environment where individuals feel valued and heard, regardless of their background or perspective. This principle encourages us to move beyond mere tolerance and actively cultivate an appreciation for the richness that comes from diverse ideas and viewpoints.

Practicing respect for the rights, beliefs, and opinions of others requires an ongoing commitment to self-awareness and empathy. It means being mindful of our own biases and limitations, and remaining open to the possibility that our understanding of the world may be incomplete. It requires humility, the willingness to listen, and the ability to engage in meaningful, respectful discourse.

In our interactions with others, we can embody this principle by actively listening to their perspectives, even when we disagree. We can strive to express our own views in a way that is respectful and considerate of differing opinions. We can also work to create spaces where individuals of all backgrounds feel safe to express themselves without fear of judgment or discrimination.

Respecting the rights, beliefs, and opinions of others is not always easy, particularly in the face of deeply held convictions or when confronted with views that challenge our own. However, it is precisely in these moments that the true test of our commitment to this principle arises. By engaging with sensitivity and understanding, even in the midst of disagreement, we contribute to the cultivation of a more inclusive and compassionate society.

Ultimately, embracing this principle serves to strengthen the fabric of our communities and promote a more peaceful and equitable world. It is a recognition of the inherent worth and dignity of each person, and a commitment to upholding these values in the way we engage with others. By respecting the rights, beliefs, and opinions of others, we contribute to the creation of a society that is grounded in empathy, understanding, and mutual respect.

CHAPTER 2

This is a key principle in upholding the foundational laws and values of a nation. The Constitution serves as the blueprint for governance, ensuring the protection of individual rights, the distribution of powers, and the establishment of the rule of law. It is crucial for citizens to actively support and defend the Constitution, as it forms the basis of a just and stable society.

The act of supporting and defending the Constitution encompasses various aspects. Firstly, it involves recognizing and respecting the rights enshrined in the Constitution, such as freedom of speech, religion, and assembly, as well as the right to due process and equal protection under the law. These rights are fundamental to preserving individual liberties and promoting a fair and inclusive society.

Moreover, supporting and defending the Constitution also entails respecting the balance of powers outlined within it. The Constitution outlines the separation of powers among the executive, legislative, and judicial branches of government to prevent any one branch from becoming too powerful. By supporting this division of powers, citizens and public officials can ensure that governance remains accountable and that decisions are made through a system of checks and balances.

Additionally, supporting and defending the Constitution involves upholding the rule of law. This means that all individuals, including government officials, are subject to the law and that legal processes are followed to ensure fairness and justice. When citizens actively support and adhere to the rule of law, they contribute to the overall stability and credibility of the legal system.

In essence, supporting and defending the Constitution is an ongoing commitment to preserving the values and principles upon which a nation is built. It requires citizens to actively engage in civil discourse, participate in democratic processes, and hold officials accountable for upholding the Constitution. By doing so, individuals contribute to the maintenance of a just and equitable society where the rule of law and individual rights are upheld.

CHAPTER 3

Respect And Obey Federal, State, And Local Laws:

it is essential for individuals to recognize the significance of legal compliance at all levels of governance. Laws serve as the framework for maintaining order, resolving disputes, and advancing the common good within a society. As such, showing respect for and obeying federal, state, and local laws is crucial for fostering a functioning and harmonious community.

Respecting and obeying federal laws entails acknowledging the authority of the national government and adhering to the legal provisions set forth by federal legislation. This includes compliance with statutes pertaining to national security, immigration, interstate commerce, and more. By recognizing the importance of federal laws, individuals contribute to a cohesive and united national framework that supports the well-being of all citizens.

Similarly, respecting and obeying state laws is essential for upholding governance at a more local level. State laws encompass a wide range of issues, including education, public safety, and healthcare, that directly impact the lives of residents within a specific state. Adhering to these laws ensures that the unique needs and priorities of individual states are addressed and that communities can flourish within the boundaries of their state-specific legal framework.

Finally, demonstrating respect for and obeying local laws is vital for ensuring the smooth functioning of neighborhoods and communities. Local laws cover various aspects of day-to-day life, including zoning regulations, business permits, and public ordinances. By abiding by these laws, individuals contribute to a safe, orderly, and pleasant living environment for themselves and their neighbors.

In conclusion, showing respect for and obeying federal, state, and local laws is integral to promoting a well-ordered society. By recognizing the significance of legal compliance at all levels of governance, individuals play a vital role in upholding the rule of law and contributing to the overall stability and prosperity of their communities.

<u>CHAPTER 4</u>

Participate In The Democratic

Process:

is a civic duty we all share. Every eligible voter isn't just entitled to a voice in our democracy, but also has the power and responsibility to shape our nation's future. By engaging in informed, thoughtful, and respectful dialogue about our different values, beliefs, and opinions, we can build a collective understanding toward working together.

Voting is the most powerful action we can take toward ensuring our democratic process works for all. When we show up to the polls, we cast our ballot to hold our elected officials accountable, ensure civil rights and liberties are protected, and protect the betterment of our nation. No matter our age, race, gender, religion, disability, or political affiliation, each of us must have our voices heard.

We can make a difference in the decisions that are made in our government. By participating in the democratic process, we're showing our respect for the U.S. Constitution, our commitment to protecting the ideals upon which this nation was founded upon, and our investment in contributing to the betterment of our society.

Let us all take our civic responsibility seriously and make sure to participate in the democratic process by voting in elections, learning about the issues, and speaking out when we see injustice. Our votes are more powerful when used collectively to create lasting change.

CHAPTER 5

Pay Income And Other Taxes Honestly, And On Time:

Another important part of being a responsible citizen. Taxes are one of the most basic obligations of citizens in a country, and must be taken seriously. There are a variety of taxes that citizens has to pay—income taxes, property taxes, sales taxes, etc. All these taxes should be paid honestly, accurately, and on time. Failing to do so can result in financial penalties or even legal repercussions.

Making sure taxes are paid honestly and on time is important not just for legal purposes but also economically. Properly collected taxes can provide much needed resources for various public projects, and help maintain a sustainable economy. Taxes also help create a sense of responsibility in citizens, as it shows that everyone contributes to the well-being of the nation.

Therefore, it's important for every citizen to pay their income and other taxes honestly, accurately, and on time. This not only is an act of good citizenship but also helps promote economic stability.

CHAPTER 6

Serve On Juries When Called Upon:

It is universally accepted that citizens who are called upon to serve on juries have a civic duty to uphold the integrity of the judicial system. Jury duty is one of the most important responsibilities of being a citizen of a democracy, and jurors play a vital role in deciding the outcomes of legal trials.

Jury duty can be a difficult and time-consuming task, but it is also a unique opportunity for citizens to take part in shaping our legal system. By entering a jury room, citizens are able to display their respect for the laws that govern our nation and uphold the values of justice and fairness that form the foundation of our society.

When called upon, citizens should have no reservations about fulfilling their jury duty.

It is an obligation to ourselves and to those around us that must be taken seriously. By giving our full attention to proceedings and by keeping an open mind, jurors can ensure that justice is done in our courts. Jury duty is a chance to do our part in making sure that our legal system is one that serves the best interests of the wider public.Paying income and other taxes honestly and on time is an important part of being a responsible citizen. Taxes are one of the most basic obligations of citizens in a country, and must be taken seriously. There are a variety of taxes that citizens has to pay—income taxes, property taxes, sales taxes, etc. All these taxes should be paid honestly, accurately, and on time. Failing to do so can result in financial penalties or even legal repercussions.

Making sure taxes are paid honestly and on time is important not just for legal purposes but also economically. Properly collected taxes can provide much needed resources for various public projects, and help maintain a sustainable economy. Taxes also help create a sense of responsibility in citizens, as it shows that everyone contributes to the well-being of the nation.

Therefore, it's important for every citizen to pay their income and other taxes honestly, accurately, and on time. This not only is an act of good citizenship but also helps promote economic stability.

CHAPTER 7

Serve In The Military Or Defense

Forces When Needed:

In the modern world, it is more important than ever to be prepared militarily and to serve in the defense forces when the need arises. The world is facing a range of security and humanitarian threats, from terrorism to pandemics, and it is essential that nations are able to respond to any of these threats when they arise. Serving in the military or defense forces is a great way to do your part to help protect your nation and the world at large. Not only do you gain valuable experience in conflict management and military tactics, but you also help to deter potential threats and ensure the safety of your fellow citizens. It is important to recognize, however, that service in the military or defense forces should not be taken lightly. It is a serious commitment that requires dedicated preparation and a willingness to put yourself in harm's way. Being educated and informed about the nature of national security and its importance is essential before committing to the military or defense forces.

CHAPTER 8

Respect The Flag And National Anthem:

is an important aspect of showing reverence and honor for the nation and its values. The flag and national anthem symbolize the unity, pride, and history of a nation and its people.

The flag is not just a piece of cloth; it is a representation of the ideals and principles that a nation stands for. When we look at the flag, we see the sacrifices made by countless individuals to uphold the values of freedom, justice, and equality. It is a symbol of national unity and resilience, reminding us of the struggles and triumphs that have shaped the nation.

Respecting the national anthem goes hand in hand with honoring the flag. When the national anthem is played or sung, it is an opportunity for all citizens to come together in unity and respect for the values enshrined in the anthem. It is a moment to reflect on the sacrifices of those who have defended the nation and its freedoms. Showing respect during the national anthem demonstrates a commitment to honoring the nation and those who have served it.

We must recognize the significance of these national symbols and the values they represent. Respecting the flag and national anthem is not just a matter of etiquette; it is a demonstration of our commitment to the principles of freedom, liberty, and justice for all. It is a way to honor the sacrifices of those who have fought to defend these ideals and to ensure that they endure for future generations.

There are many ways to demonstrate respect for the flag and national anthem. Standing at attention and facing the flag during the national anthem, removing headgear, and placing the right hand over the heart are all gestures of respect. It is important to participate in these acts with sincerity and solemnity, recognizing the significance of the moment.

It is also important to honor the flag by ensuring it is displayed and maintained with dignity and care. The flag should be treated with respect and never allowed to touch the ground. When flying the flag, it should be done so with proper etiquette, following guidelines on when and how to display it.

In conclusion, respecting the flag and national anthem is not just a symbolic gesture; it is a way to honor the nation and the values it represents. By showing respect for these national symbols, we affirm our commitment to the principles of freedom, equality, and justice that they embody. It is a way to show appreciation for the sacrifices of those who have defended these values and to uphold the unity and pride of the nation.

CHAPTER 9

Vote In Local, State, And National Elections:

is a fundamental right and a civic responsibility that is essential for a healthy democracy. The act of voting is an opportunity for every citizen to have a say in the governance of their community, state, and nation. It is a way to ensure that the voices of the people are heard and that their interests are represented by those in power.

Participating in elections at all levels of government is crucial for several reasons.

First and foremost, it is a means for individuals to have a direct impact on the policies and decisions that affect their lives. By casting a vote, citizens can influence the direction of their communities, states, and the nation as a whole. It is a way for the people to hold their elected officials accountable and shape the future of their society.

Furthermore, voting is a way to ensure that the government reflects the diversity and interests of the population. When citizens from all walks of life participate in the electoral process, it provides a more accurate representation of the needs and aspirations of the entire populace. It is through voting that individuals can advocate for change and progress in their communities and beyond.

In addition to its impact on policy and representation, voting is a means of safeguarding democracy itself. By participating in elections, citizens contribute to the preservation of the democratic principles that underpin the nation's governance. Voting is an embodiment of the idea that power ultimately resides in the hands of the people, and it is a way to reaffirm the democratic values of equality and participation.

While the importance of voting is clear, it is essential to recognize that this right has been hard-won through the struggles of many who fought for the right to participate in the democratic process. Many individuals have faced significant barriers, discrimination, and even violence in their efforts to secure the right to vote. Therefore, it is imperative to honor their sacrifices by exercising the right to vote.

To ensure that voting is accessible to all citizens, it is crucial to promote voter education and registration initiatives. Providing accurate information about the voting process, the candidates, and the issues at stake is vital for empowering individuals to make informed decisions at the ballot box. Efforts to remove obstacles to voting, such as long lines, limited polling places, and discriminatory practices, are also essential for upholding the integrity of the electoral process.

In conclusion, voting in local, state, and national elections is a cornerstone of democracy and a responsibility that should be embraced by all citizens. By participating in the electoral process, individuals have the power to shape the course of their communities, states, and the nation. It is a way to honor the sacrifices of those who fought for this right and to ensure that the voices of the people continue to guide the course of the nation's governance.

CHAPTER 10

Respect The National Symbols Of

The United States:

the national anthem, and other emblems, hold significant meaning and represent the values, history, and unity of the nation. Respecting these symbols is essential for fostering a sense of patriotism, unity, and reverence for the ideals that the United States stands for.

The flag of the United States, with its stars and stripes, is a powerful symbol of the nation's history and principles. It represents the unity of the states, the courage of those who have defended the nation, and the ideals of freedom and equality. When we see the flag flying, it serves as a reminder of the sacrifices made to secure and uphold the nation's values.

Respecting the flag means treating it with the dignity and honor it deserves. This includes displaying the flag properly and in good condition, observing proper etiquette when the flag is raised, lowered, or passing, and never allowing it to touch the ground. Respecting the flag also involves demonstrating reverence during the national anthem, standing at attention, facing the flag, and placing the right hand over the heart as a gesture of respect.

The national anthem, "The Star-Spangled Banner," holds a special place among the national symbols of the United States. Its stirring lyrics recount the resilience of the nation during times of peril and the enduring spirit of freedom. When the national anthem is played or sung, it is an opportunity for all citizens to come together and reflect on the nation's values and sacrifices, demonstrating respect for the unity and pride of the nation.

In addition to the flag and national anthem, other symbols such as the bald eagle, the Great Seal of the United States, and the Pledge of Allegiance are significant representations of the nation's heritage and values. These symbols serve as reminders of the nation's history, the principles it was built upon, and the ongoing pursuit of liberty and justice for all.

Respecting the national symbols of the United States is not just a matter of custom or tradition; it is a way to honor the nation and the values it stands for. It is a demonstration of reverence for the sacrifices made by those who have defended the nation and its freedoms, as well as a commitment to upholding the unity and pride of the country.

It is important to educate future generations about the significance of these national symbols and the values they represent. Teaching children and young people about the history and meaning of the flag, the national anthem, and other emblems fosters an understanding of the nation's principles and encourages a sense of patriotism and unity.

In conclusion, respecting the national symbols of the United States is an essential aspect of fostering a deep sense of patriotism, pride, and unity. By showing reverence for the flag, the national anthem, and other emblems, we honor the nation's history and values, and reaffirm our commitment to upholding the principles of freedom, equality, and justice for all. It is a way to demonstrate gratitude for the sacrifices of those who have defended the nation and to ensure that these symbols continue to inspire and unite the people of the United States.

CHAPTER 11

is essential in a democratic society, as it allows individuals to make well-informed decisions and engage in civil discourse. In today's world, it is crucial to stay updated on local, national, and global events, including politics, social issues, environmental concerns, and more. This can be achieved by following reputable news sources, engaging in discussions with people from diverse backgrounds, and critically assessing different perspectives.

Participating in civil discourse involves engaging in respectful and constructive conversations about important issues. It means listening with an open mind, acknowledging differing viewpoints, and expressing your own thoughts in a considerate manner. By actively participating in civil discourse, individuals can contribute to a more informed and empathetic society, where meaningful dialogue leads to positive change and understanding.

In a society where disagreements are inevitable, civil discourse serves as a crucial tool for fostering mutual respect, empathy, and understanding. It enables people to confront societal challenges, address conflicts, and work toward viable solutions. By embracing civil discourse, individuals can bridge ideological divides and cultivate an environment where diverse perspectives are valued and respected.

CHAPTER 12

Volunteer In Causes Which Are Important To You:

Volunteering in causes that are important to you not only allows you to contribute to the betterment of society but also provides personal fulfillment and a sense of purpose. Whether it's advocating for environmental conservation, supporting underprivileged communities, or promoting education, volunteering offers a meaningful way to make a positive impact. It allows individuals to align their values with their actions, creating a more cohesive and compassionate society.

Volunteering provides an opportunity to connect with like-minded individuals and build a strong network of supporters who share a common cause. By dedicating your time and skills to a cause that resonates with you, you can inspire others to join in and amplify the impact of your efforts. Additionally, volunteering exposes you to new perspectives, experiences, and challenges, which can contribute to personal growth and development.

Furthermore, volunteering can have a profound effect on the communities and individuals you aim to assist. It can help address social, environmental, or health-related issues, providing tangible support to those in need. By actively engaging in volunteer work, individuals can become catalysts for positive change and contribute to the creation of a more inclusive and compassionate society.

CHAPTER 13

Be Informed About The History, Cultures, And Customs Of The United States:

is essential for fostering mutual respect, empathy, and unity among its people. By familiarizing oneself with the nation's past, including significant historical events, cultural traditions, and the experiences of various ethnic and social groups, individuals can cultivate a deeper appreciation for the country's complexities and diversity.

Moreover, learning about the history, cultures, and customs of the United States allows individuals to gain a broader perspective on the challenges and triumphs that have shaped the nation. It provides insight into the struggles and achievements of different communities, fostering empathy and understanding across cultural boundaries. This knowledge can serve as a foundation for meaningful interactions and collaborations across diverse groups.

By embracing a nuanced understanding of the United States' history, cultures, and customs, individuals can actively contribute to the promotion of inclusivity, equality, and social cohesion. It enables people to

engage in informed discussions, challenge
stereotypes, and celebrate the
contributions of various cultural groups,
ultimately fostering a more interconnected
and harmonious society.

CHAPTER 14

And Lastly, Be A Good Neighbor And Participate In Your Community:

cultivates a sense of belonging, support, and cooperation among individuals. Engaging with your neighbors fosters a strong sense of community, promotes social cohesion, and creates an environment where people look out for one another. By building positive relationships with your neighbors, you contribute to a more connected and supportive local community.

Participating in your community can take many forms, from volunteering for local initiatives to joining community organizations or attending neighborhood gatherings. By actively engaging in community activities, individuals can contribute to the creation of a vibrant and inclusive local environment, where diverse voices are heard and valued. Taking an active role in shaping your community allows you to have a direct impact on its development and well-being.

Furthermore, being a good neighbor involves showing empathy, consideration, and support for those around you. It means lending a helping hand, offering support to those in need, and fostering a spirit of mutual aid within your community. By participating in acts of kindness and cooperation, individuals can contribute to the creation of a nurturing and compassionate community where everyone feels valued and included.

In summary, being informed about important issues, volunteering, understanding the history and cultures of the United States, and being an active participant in your community are all crucial aspects of being a responsible and engaged member of society. Embracing these principles fosters empathy, respect, and cooperation, leading to a more connected, inclusive, and supportive society for all.

CONCLUSION

In conclusion, the principles outlined - to respect the rights, beliefs, and opinions of others; to support and defend the Constitution; to obey the laws; to participate in the democratic process; to fulfill tax obligations; to serve on juries and in the military when needed; to respect national symbols; to vote in elections; to be informed and engage in civil discourse; to volunteer; to understand the history and culture of the United States; and to be a good neighbor and community participant - are all essential components of responsible citizenship. Embracing these values promotes a society based on mutual respect, civic engagement, and a shared commitment to upholding the principles upon which the nation was founded. By adhering to these guidelines, individuals contribute to the strength and vitality of their communities and foster a spirit of unity and cooperation that is integral to the continued success of the nation.

<u>YOUR MEMORY NOTE</u>

YOUR MEMORY NOTE

<u>YOUR MEMORY NOTE</u>

YOUR MEMORY NOTE

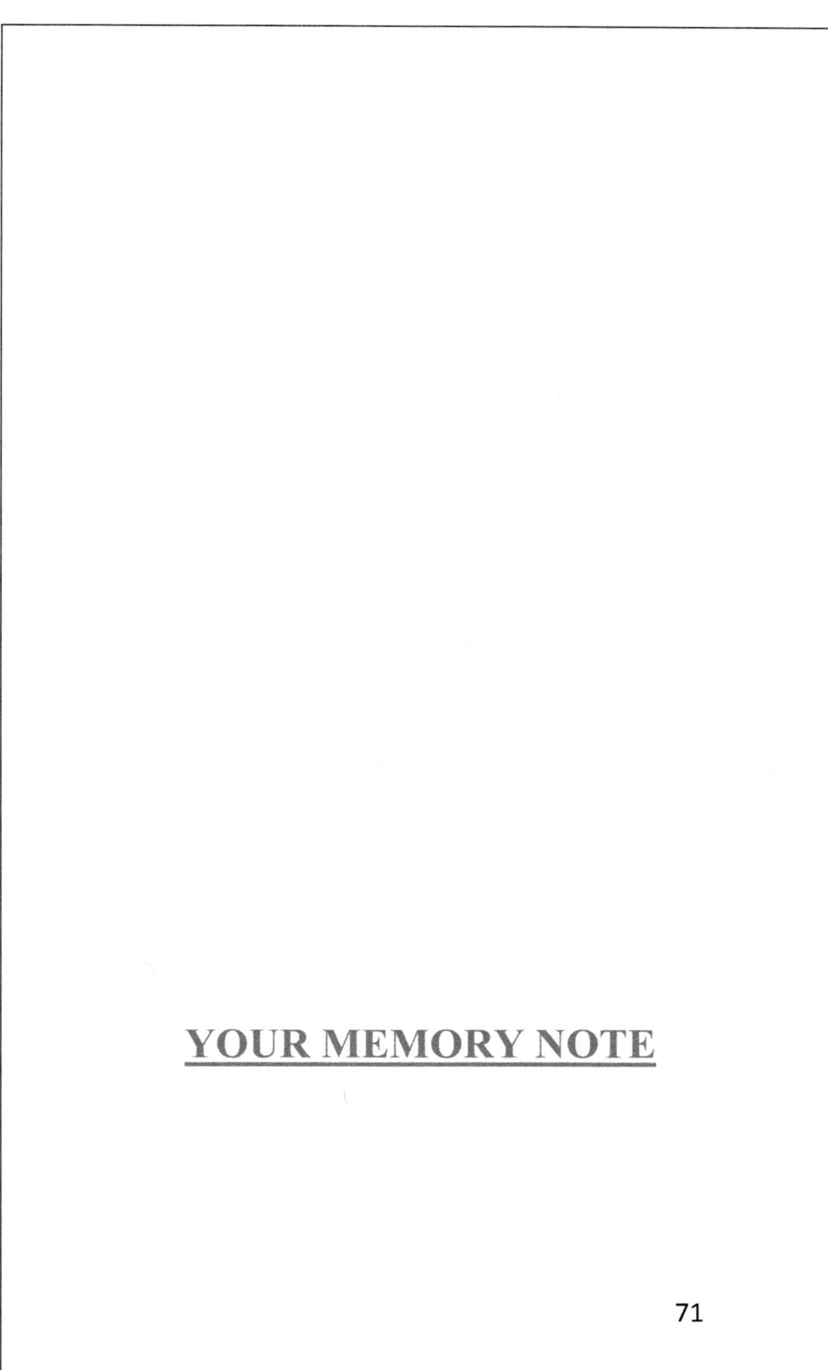

YOUR MEMORY NOTE